IN THE
NATIONAL INTEREST

General Sir John Monash once exhorted a graduating class to 'equip yourself for life, not solely for your own benefit but for the benefit of the whole community'. At the university established in his name, we repeat this statement to our own graduating classes, to acknowledge how important it is that common or public good flows from education.

Universities spread and build on the knowledge they acquire through scholarship in many ways, well beyond the transmission of this learning through education. It is a necessary part of a university's role to debate its findings, not only with other researchers and scholars, but also with the broader community in which it resides.

Publishing for the benefit of society is an important part of a university's commitment to free intellectual inquiry. A university provides civil space for such inquiry by its scholars, as well as for investigations by public intellectuals and expert practitioners.

This series, In the National Interest, embodies Monash University's mission to extend knowledge and encourage informed debate about matters of great significance to Australia's future.

Professor Margaret Gardner AC
President and Vice-Chancellor,
Monash University

PAUL FLETCHER
GOVERNING IN THE INTERNET AGE

MONASH
UNIVERSITY
PUBLISHING

Governing in the Internet Age
© Copyright 2021 Paul Fletcher

Monash University Publishing
Matheson Library Annexe
40 Exhibition Walk
Monash University
Clayton, Victoria 3800, Australia
https://publishing.monash.edu

Monash University Publishing brings to the world publications which advance the best traditions of humane and enlightened thought.

ISBN: 9781922464804 (paperback)
ISBN: 9781922464811 (ebook)

Series: In the National Interest
Editor: Louise Adler
Project manager & copyeditor: Paul Smitz
Designer: Peter Long
Typesetter: Cannon Typesetting
Proofreader: Gillian Armitage
Printed in Australia by Ligare Book Printers

A catalogue record for this book is available from the National Library of Australia.

GOVERNING IN THE INTERNET AGE

In just thirty years, the internet has brought extraordinary change.

It has changed the way we find and consume news, books, music, television and movies; the way we do our banking and our shopping; the way we exercise, find recipes and make our meals; the way we find and book restaurants, accommodation, flights and travel.

It has changed the way we choose a route when walking, driving or using other forms of transport; the way we find partners for life—or for one night; the way we keep public records, find information, access collections in libraries and research family history.

It has changed the way we record, store and transport data. It has changed the way we control large infrastructure and utility systems, and the way we monitor and control our domestic power usage.

It has changed the way we track animals and measure soil moisture on farms. It has changed the way we look for a job and the way we work.

It has changed the way we promote ourselves, our businesses and our causes.

It has changed the way we keep in touch with friends and family.

In fact, it has fundamentally changed the way we do just about everything.

When the internet first came along, it caught governments unaware. As it roared out of the labs and into everyday life, as the number of people online rose from millions to tens of millions and then into the hundreds of millions and then billions—all in a few short years—governments struggled to keep up. That period is behind us. Governments are now much more confident in the way they respond to the internet.

Of course, plenty of policy challenges remain. While the internet has introduced new ways of serving citizens, and new opportunities for communicating and informing, it has engendered new social problems and also prompted new economic policy concerns, especially with domestic businesses facing global, internet-based competitors. And governments, not unreasonably, are expected to competently address all these issues. What good government looks like in the age of the internet is the focus of this book.

WHAT, EXACTLY, HAS CHANGED?

Let us start by looking at precisely what has changed over the past thirty years. It is not just that almost every computer around the world is now connected to a network. We have also seen the arrival, and explosion, of mobile telephony; the deregulation of telecommunications in many countries; the invention of the smartphone; and the transition from narrow-band to broadband internet. Multiple, different innovations in different fields—technical, commercial, regulatory—have come together to have a profound collective impact, transforming the way humans connect with each other and do so many things that rely on the exchange of information. The development of the internet is just one part of this story.

As early as the 1960s, researchers for the US Defense Department developed the idea of 'packet switching'. In order for data to be sent from one place to another, it would be broken down into small 'packets', each with a header giving vital information, including the address to which it was to be delivered. These 'packets' could travel to their destinations across many different physical routes, whereupon they would be recombined in the right order, using the header. Why was such a complicated approach devised? Among other reasons, it was so that networks could still be used even if some physical links had been destroyed; for example, in a nuclear war. If any physical routes existed, the packets would find them and travel over them.

In the 1980s, Tim Berners-Lee, a British physicist working at a research laboratory in Europe, developed a method of connecting many different computers around the world. Harnessing the packet-switching approach, Berners-Lee's software allowed the user of one computer to access data on another computer. Devices using this software were joined up into a 'world wide web'. In the early days, this 'web' consisted of a few thousand computers at research laboratories and universities. But in the 1990s it began to emerge into the public realm, thanks to the development of the internet browser. No longer was it necessary to enter complex terms in a programming language to access data on the World Wide Web; the internet could now be used by all of us.

As the world of computing technology changed, so did the commercial structure of the telecommunications industry. For a century, the telephone networks in most countries had been run by government-owned monopolies. That began to change from the 1980s, as British Telecom, Telecom Australia, Telecom New Zealand, Telia in Sweden and Deutsche Telekom in Germany, along with their counterparts in many other countries, were sold into private hands and competitors were allowed into the market as well. The result was more innovation and lower prices. In turn, that meant it was not just technically possible to send data over telecommunications networks between computers in many different physical locations—it was also now economically possible for companies and even individuals to do so.

At the same time, computers were getting smaller and more powerful. The first IBM personal computer came onto the market in 1981 using an operating system developed by a young programming genius from Seattle named Bill Gates. By the end of the decade, laptop computers were small enough to carry into meetings. Before too long, mobile networks and wireless modems meant you could take your laptop on the road and remain connected to your office.

In the mid-1990s, households in advanced economies like Australia began connecting to the internet. In 1996, some 286 000 households were connected in Australia;[1] by 2000 it was 2.3 million households;[2] and by 2016 it was 88 per cent of the Australian population.[3] Internet speeds also advanced rapidly, and within a few years, dial-up or 'narrowband' internet had been supplanted by broadband. In the 1990s, a typical home internet service ran at 56 kilobits per second—definitely narrowband!—but a decade later, many households were getting 5 megabits per second

(Mbps), a hundred times faster. Today, three-quarters of customers on the National Broadband Network have a 50 Mbps or higher plan, a thousand times faster than those 1990s speeds.

Another big change over this period was the arrival of mobile phones. In 1990, they were an expensive luxury that hardly anyone could afford: there was roughly one mobile phone for every 100 Australians. Nine years later, it was forty mobile phones per 100 Australians, and by 2017, three-quarters of Australians owned a smartphone.[4] Mobile phones started off offering only voice services. But by the late 1990s we had become big users of the short messaging service. It is hard to believe today, but before 1999 in Australia, you could only send an SMS to a customer on the same network. Once cross-platform SMS arrived, usage took off.[5]

Social behaviours began to alter as we started to use SMS to communicate with friends and family as well as for work. Instead of making a phone call, we could send an SMS birthday greeting or fire off a quick text to say we were running late. Businesses started texting customers to remind them about upcoming appointments. The practice proved to be very convenient and popular—and it was an indication of how, in a world where everybody is connected, the way we interact changes significantly.

The second-generation mobile services that brought us SMS began to look outdated when third-generation or 3G mobile came along. It was launched in Australia by Hutchison Telecommunications in 2003 under the brand name '3'. For the first time, high-speed data could be sent over a mobile phone, and very soon people realised their phone directly connected them to the internet and the immense amount of information it offered. But a convenient and user-friendly way of accessing and using all this information remained elusive. Many of us were overwhelmed. Every mobile phone manufacturer seemed to have its own software and tools. Nothing seemed to fit together very easily.

That changed in 2007 when Apple introduced the iPhone. It took existing technologies—including 3G mobile communications—and packaged them into one well-designed, user-friendly device. For one thing, the iPhone introduced most of us to video-calling. The device combined the FaceTime app with an inbuilt camera, screen and microphone, and thanks to the bandwidth available over 3G networks, video-calling became widely available to consumers.

The past thirty years, then, have seen several remarkable sets of innovations occurring simultaneously. This extraordinary technology is part of everyday life for a huge number of people across the world: more than five billion have mobile phones, and an estimated 4.72 billion are connected to the internet.[6]

The American economist Robert J Gordon argues that the single most significant period of technological innovation in history was the nineteenth century. It brought us electricity, plumbing and sewerage, refrigeration and air conditioning, the motor vehicle and many other technologies. According to Gordon, the internet allows us to do things more cheaply and conveniently, but if you had a choice between going back to a world without electricity, plumbing and the car, or living in a world without the internet, you would probably give up the internet more readily.[7]

Perhaps that is right, although it is a somewhat artificial thought experiment. But even if other technological changes have had bigger impacts on how humans live, there is no doubt the change brought by the internet has already been enormous.

Consider some of the things that have changed in just a few decades. Information is now abundant, available everywhere, and just about free. With a $200 smartphone, you can connect to the internet and instantly get information on just about any topic of interest to you. Of course, there is also an abundance of junk, and much of what is online cannot be verified. But reliable government, academic and civil society sources of information abound, as well as huge volumes of teaching material from reputable universities and other institutions.

A really important change is that a consumer today is so much better equipped than twenty or thirty years ago. Price-comparison sites make it much easier to avoid being ripped off. Shopping online, you can quickly see what is available, and compare prices and features. It used to take time and effort to check the price of a good or service at different shops; today, it can be done in seconds. And if you do not like what is on offer from merchants in your own city or country, you can order online from sellers all around the world. In addition, many products and services that essentially consist of data—books, movies, records, financial services—can be purchased and consumed online without the customer ever needing to go to a physical store.

One of the biggest changes can be seen in the way humans now communicate and interact with each other. No matter how specialised your interest, you can connect online with people who share it, all around the world. No longer are you restricted to people you meet at your school or work or in your neighbourhood.

These are extraordinary changes. But, as with any major innovation, the global transition to the internet age has brought us new problems. Should we be concerned about the many unproductive hours spent scrolling through social media? How do we address the problem of online trolls spewing hate? Or the risk we face online of being ripped off by criminals and confidence tricksters who may be operating anywhere in the world? Governments have a duty to keep their citizens safe, so there is new, ever-evolving work for them to do in identifying and responding to the pitfalls and risks that are part of internet use.

For example, governments enforce laws concerning privacy and defamation. This is now much more complicated in a world where just about anybody can make a statement that can be seen, at least theoretically, by billions of people. A country's government also sets the laws that must be followed by anybody doing business in that country. But today, an internet-based business can sell products and services in very large numbers all around the world. It is not straightforward for a national government to assert its sovereignty and legal power over a global online business that may have no physical assets or employees in the country, and that may structure its internal arrangements and transfer pricing so there is no profit recorded in that country.

These complexities, challenges and opportunities—coupled with the extraordinarily rapid growth of the internet—have left governments on the back foot for much of the past thirty years. But the evidence suggests that governments are beginning to do a much better job in their response to the internet. Weighing up that evidence means considering a series of questions: What has been the impact of the internet on the sovereignty of nation-states, including smaller countries like Australia? How should we regulate content and conduct in the online environment? What does the internet mean for both consumers and businesses in a competitive digital global world? It also points to some principles that governments should apply in the internet age.

THE INTERNET AND THE SOVEREIGNTY OF NATION-STATES

On 18 February 2021, Australians awoke to learn that the Facebook pages of many businesses and organisations were not working. *The Sydney Morning Herald*, Nine News, the ABC and *The Australian* were just some of the many well-known media organisations that were 'off the air'. But the impact was much wider than that. Fire, police and ambulance services, rape crisis centres, and local Facebook groups—including North Shore Mums, a business in my electorate of Bradfield—also had their Facebook pages taken down.

Over seventeen million Australians use Facebook every day, and so the sudden removal of these pages and the ensuing disruption was shocking to many. Who could have carried out such a hostile act?

Many Australians were surprised to learn that it was Facebook itself that had taken this action. Across the community, people expressed their frustration and anger. What was going on?

Facebook's dramatic act was in protest over a new law the Australian Government was about to pass: the News Media Bargaining Code. This law gave Australian news media businesses the right to negotiate with the digital platforms Google and Facebook, to agree on remuneration when those platforms used content generated and paid for by one of those businesses. For example, if a two-minute video clip from Nine News appeared in a Facebook post, Facebook would need to make a payment to Nine. The social media giant decided to retaliate by preventing content from Australian news media businesses from appearing on its site. It quickly conceded, though, that it had blocked too wide a range of pages, including from many organisations which were not news media business entities and were not covered by the new law. Facebook scrambled to reopen these pages, but it had already done significant damage to its brand.

Within days the issue was resolved, following intense negotiations between Treasurer Josh Frydenberg and Facebook CEO Mark Zuckerberg. The new law was passed, with support across all political parties. Facebook's attempt at intimidating the Australian Government had backfired. Google had also contested the new code, saying it was considering withdrawing its search engine from Australia, but ultimately it, too, backtracked on its threat.

Some regard this episode as evidence that global internet behemoths such as Facebook and Google are a threat to the sovereignty of nation-states. Commentator Terry McCrann wrote in *The Australian*:

> The battle with Google is a battle that Australia just cannot afford to lose. To stress, I'm saying that it's a—actually, utterly seminal—battle that Australia must not lose. Not Australian media, or even specific media outlets like this paper or its owner News Corp, but the country overall, assuming we are a country that values having some control over itself and its future.[8]

I see it differently, as evidence that the relationship between sovereign governments and internet businesses is gradually normalising. Ten years ago, I think that Facebook and Google might well have won this stand-off. But governments everywhere are fighting back, and the special treatment internet businesses have enjoyed since the 1990s is coming to an end.

It has taken a while. In the early years of the internet, advocates sought to position it as existing beyond the sovereignty of nation-states. In 1996, US cyberlibertarian and poet John Perry Barlow issued his 'Declaration of the Independence of Cyberspace':

> Governments of the Industrial World, you weary giants of flesh and steel, I come from Cyberspace, the new home of Mind. On behalf of the future, I ask you of the past to leave us alone. You are not welcome among us. You have no sovereignty where we gather.[9]

The idea of an internet beyond the reach of government might have been tenable while it was a specialised resource used by a small number of researchers and academics. But it became increasingly difficult to sustain once the internet became a mass-market consumer phenomenon.

Nation-states zealously guard their sovereignty. No government—authoritarian or democratic—will simply stand by and allow that sovereignty to be eroded. Authoritarian governments are unlikely to support a medium that allows their citizens to freely communicate, inform themselves, transact and do many other things without government oversight. Democratically elected governments—like Australia's—make rules governing the conduct of citizens in their jurisdiction, their right to do so based on the legitimacy acquired at the ballot box. They also respond to the expectations of citizens, and in the online world, that includes the desire for order to be maintained and for personal safety to be protected.

When people interact in the physical town square, they take it for granted the rule of law applies. If they are assaulted or defrauded, or otherwise harmed, they can go to the police and seek assistance, or they can go to court and seek redress. As the internet took hold, it quickly became apparent people anticipated the same thing when they interacted in the digital town square.

I remember, some years ago, joining an education session for parents, held at a school in my electorate, on the risks their children faced online. I spoke briefly at the start, but most of the session consisted of the parents listening to a presentation from an expert on the topic, followed by questions and group discussion. One parent explained that photos taken at a party of her drunken teenage son had been posted on social media. Could they be taken down, and what might it mean when the boy went for a job, she wondered. The presenter explained there was not much that could be done, as the site's terms of use gave it complete discretion about how the photos were used. I still remember this woman turning to me, incredulous, and saying, 'Paul, that can't be right! How can the government allow that?'

Most Australians would simply expect, as she did, that the Australian Government can make and enforce laws about what Australians do online. But there is considerable tension between this assumption and the global nature of the internet—this borderless collection of computers and the data that travel over them, accessible by people around the world. Indeed, as the internet has grown, there has been an ongoing battle between online businesses and governments about whether, and how, those businesses should be regulated. The arguments against regulation have come in many forms, including the cyberlibertarian premise that the internet should be beyond the reach of sovereign nations, which I mentioned earlier. But when a democratically elected government confronts the expectations of citizens that they—or even more viscerally, their children—will be kept safe, such philosophical niceties do not last long.

One argument routinely used by big internet businesses is that if the Australian Government imposes local laws on them, Australia will risk becoming a technological backwater. In 2014, for example, the Australian Government proposed setting up a new body to regulate certain content online: the Children's eSafety Commissioner. The Australian Interactive Media Industry Association, at the time the peak body representing companies such as Google, Facebook and Microsoft, resisted fiercely, saying in a submission that it had

> serious practical concerns with the proposed policy: a rapid take down scheme will at best take five days (much longer than [the] industry's own processes), [and there is] the possibility that the policy will push children to undertake risky behaviour [on] platforms with less highly developed self-regulatory standards and significant likelihood that the laws will be unable to keep pace with technological change.[10]

Whether or not there is a philosophical basis for it, the global internet giants have consistently fought aggressively against government laws which they see as going against their economic interests.

In 2018, the Australian Government changed the law to remove an exemption from the goods and services tax that had previously applied to online transactions with a value below $1000.[11] We did this because the exemption gave global internet businesses an unfair advantage over Australian businesses that were their competitors—when a consumer faced a choice between buying a television in a department store or buying the same television online, they would discover that the former purchase attracted GST (and hence would cost the customer more) and the latter did not. Amazon, the global ecommerce giant, protested strongly. In fact, Amazon withdrew its services from Australia for about six months before choosing to comply with the new law and re-enter the market.

In other words, the resistance shown by Facebook and Google in 2021 to the Australian Government's News Media Bargaining Code was very much in line with similar resistance by internet businesses to other proposed laws in this country over the last thirty years. There is nothing inherently unusual about big businesses working to protect their economic interests, but the global internet firms have some unusual features that add to the challenge they represent to the sovereignty of nation-states.

One is their sheer scale. Locally, they have a very big presence in the market—each month, over nineteen million Australians use Google Search and over seventeen million use Facebook.[12] Globally, they are very large, operating in a hundred or so countries, and they are very profitable: Google's market capitalisation is around US$1.6 trillion, while Facebook's is nearly US$860 billion.

Another feature is the intangible nature of the services they provide. On the one hand, these services allow them to compete very effectively for advertising revenue with Australian businesses such as News Corporation and Nine Entertainment Limited. Over the past twenty years, as Google and Facebook have steadily expanded, traditional media businesses have just as steadily lost advertising revenue—the money earned by metropolitan commercial television broadcasters through agency bookings declined by more than 30 per cent in the ten years to September 2020.[13] Today, Google dominates the market for digital advertising in Australia. According to the Australian Competition & Consumer Commission, Google's revenue share of the digital advertising market ranges from 50–60 per cent to 90–100 per cent, depending on the required service.[14]

On the other hand, the intangible nature of their services means that Google and Facebook can largely avoid paying tax here. While these corporations earn billions each year in Australia, for tax purposes, most of that ends up as income booked in the low-tax jurisdictions of Singapore and Ireland. Television and radio networks, newspapers and other traditional media businesses, by contrast, earn their revenues in Australia and pay tax at the statutory rate of 30 per cent on their profits. So, as these businesses have lost advertising revenue to Google and Facebook, in turn this has meant a loss of tax revenue for the Australian Government.

A further feature is that the Australia-based management of both Facebook and Google have little autonomy: the important decisions are made in California. Facebook's head office, for example, makes internationally binding decisions about things like the minimum age at which you can have an account; the kind of content that can be posted, and what user guidelines it is subject to; and when your account can be suspended or closed. In the past, any attempt by governments in Australia to impose regulatory requirements on the operation of the digital giants has been met with great resistance.

Of course, there are plenty of global businesses operating in Australia, in a whole range of industries. That is not of itself a challenge to sovereignty. But what has distinguished the internet businesses, I would argue, is that for much of the past thirty years they have been able to persuade governments they are somehow different to other sectors, and should not face regulatory obligations of the sort that most other businesses have long accepted.

I think there are several reasons why they have been able to do that. The first is the speed at which this has all happened. As I pointed out earlier, in a relatively brief period, the internet has gone from being a specialised resource used by a small number of researchers to a mass-market consumer phenomenon, with nearly five billion people online around the world. It is not surprising that governments have taken a little while to respond.

A second reason is the highly decentralised nature of the internet. It is not located or controlled in any one place. Rather, it is a collection of billions of different computers—from massive supercomputers in academic and research institutions, to computers in millions of businesses, schools and other organisations, to the smartphones that billions of people across the world now carry. As a result, it is not at all obvious which government should take the lead in regulating when, for example, highly violent content is stored on a server in one country and seen by viewers in another country. When technology is deliberately used to make the source location unclear, or to rapidly move the content between different locations, or to host it simultaneously in multiple locations in many different countries, it is less obvious still. That said, while these were novel issues thirty years ago, they are much better understood today—and very much more the subject of regulatory focus and intergovernmental cooperation.

The third factor explaining why the online sector has been treated differently for so long, I believe, is our collective 'mental model' of the internet as a highly disaggregated construct of millions or even billions of small operations. This is the assumption behind the cyberlibertarian ideas I referenced earlier. But that is emphatically not how the internet has turned out. Instead, economic activity over the internet has evolved into a market structure where, in sector after sector, there are a small number of extremely large, globally dominant businesses which enjoy apparently ever-increasing returns to scale that make it impossible for competitors to grow in relative size. Consider the dominance in their markets of Facebook, Google, Amazon, Netflix and eBay. The idea that such behemoths should be free of regulatory oversight is completely untenable.

I argued earlier that the response to the Australian Government's News Media Bargaining Code is evidence of a gradual normalisation in the way big internet businesses are regulated. It shows the growing confidence of governments in taking on these businesses and subjecting them to the same kinds of regulatory frameworks as other organisations. In fact, if we look at the history of other technologies, we see that it generally takes time for regulation to catch up. When the motor car first came along, for example, there were no speed limits, no traffic lights, no driver's licences, no requirements for seat belts or the many other safety measures we take for granted today. Rather, there was the staged development of regulation, which we have seen repeated time after time: a new technology is developed, it is introduced, it brings benefits but also some risks, and in response governments regulate to require various protective measures against those risks. We are seeing the same pattern with the internet; we are just at an earlier point of the process.

Governments, perhaps, can be forgiven for taking some time to work out how best to regulate the new online world. But, as time has passed, they have shown increasing confidence in their efforts and ability to regulate online activity. That has certainly been the pattern in Australia.

In 1999, the *Broadcasting Services Act* was amended with the addition of a scheme to regulate online content in Australia. It provided for differential treatment of content hosted in Australia and content hosted overseas, with no capacity for the regulator to take firm action against the latter. This was based on the view at the time that attempting to impose Australian law on websites hosted overseas was a futile exercise. Over time, that view changed. In 2013, Australia chaired the discussions that led to the UN General Assembly agreeing for the first time that the law applies as much online as it does offline.

Then, in 2015, we established the world's first eSafety Commissioner, a dedicated statutory position with a mandate to keep Australians safe online. In 2017, Australia advocated for the inclusion of the online dimensions of tackling violent extremism in the G20 'Leaders' Statement on Countering Terrorism'. And in 2019, Prime Minister Scott Morrison played a key role in securing a G20 leaders' statement calling on the tech industry to do more to prevent the misuse of their platforms by terrorists.

There are those who continue to resist the regulatory reach of government, and some who still try to bluff governments into believing regulation is technically impossible or would destroy the benefits which the internet has provided. But the widely held view in the early years of the internet—that it should be beyond the realm of governments—is not seriously advanced anymore.

Facebook, Google and the other successful internet companies are enormous global businesses. Their emergence has destroyed the argument that it is neither possible nor desirable to regulate the internet. It is certainly possible when the great majority of places that consumers go to online are managed by large listed public companies based in the United States or other advanced nations. This is a fundamentally different reality to what was feared by governments at the dawn of the internet: that the typical website visited by a consumer in Australia would be hosted by a smallish business based in a near-lawless country like Syria or Yemen, and hence any attempt to subject it to Australian laws would be futile.

Over time, governments have had many bruising battles with internet businesses. But a clear lesson has emerged. When a lawfully elected government—in Australia or in any other jurisdiction—has made laws regulating the conduct of internet businesses within that jurisdiction, the sizeable US companies which do business there will comply. Certainly, before the relevant laws are finalised, these businesses will use their extensive resources to argue against such laws being made. They may well engage US diplomatic efforts to make their case. They will lobby politicians in the jurisdiction. They will use the courts to raise legal challenges. But once such laws are made and come into force—assuming they are sufficiently well drafted that they cannot be overturned in court— the internet businesses will comply. It is simply not possible to be a law-abiding global company based in the United States or a similarly developed jurisdiction and do otherwise.

It is clear, then, that it is *possible* to regulate internet businesses. The other belief that held sway in the early years of the online realm, and which similarly has not stood up well, is that it is not *desirable* to regulate internet businesses. On the contrary, I would argue that it is desirable, for the same economic policy reason that applies to the laws designed to constrain the market power of businesses in other sectors: so those businesses do not leverage their market power to destroy competition and in turn exploit consumers.

In the 1890s, the United States began to introduce laws to contain the market power of giant corporations in sectors like steel and railways: the so-called anti-trust laws. They were highly politically controversial and faced enormous pushback from the powerful and wealthy businesses in those sectors, which were strongly resistant to being regulated. But the policy logic for such regulation was very much the same as that informing efforts by today's governments to regulate global corporations like Facebook, Google and Amazon—in the face of responses from those businesses that are very similar to those of the steel, railway and oil barons of the 1890s. It is no coincidence that the laws passed by the Australian Government concerning Facebook and Google were developed by the ACCC, our regulator of market power and competition issues. Nor is it a coincidence that competition regulators in other countries have closely followed the introduction of these laws.

From today's perspective, it is easy to see how the internet has increasingly posed a challenge to the sovereignty of nation-states. And, with the benefit of hindsight, it is clear that governments were initially slow to recognise and respond to that challenge. Now, some thirty years on, governments are more confident and assertive, and the policy case for regulating online activity is widely accepted.

CONTENT AND CONDUCT, AND KEEPING CITIZENS SAFE

Almost a quarter of 18–24-year-old women in Australia have had a nude or sexual image of them posted online without their consent.[15] It is an extraordinary statistic, and a compelling example of one of the many social issues we now face because of what the internet makes possible.

Noelle Martin is a young woman who has been a victim of such image-based abuse. (I prefer the term 'image-based abuse' to 'revenge porn', a phrase which wrongly implies the victim has done something to bring humiliation upon themselves.) When Noelle discovered her face had been combined with an image of somebody else's naked body in a pornographic deepfake and posted online, she was shocked. But she fought back using her skills as a law student, campaigning for changes to the law to help victims. In 2019, she became the Young Western Australian of the Year.

When I met Noelle, she explained to me the devastating impact of such abuse on its victims, who are overwhelmingly women. What you want in this situation, more than anything else, is to get the images taken down. The idea that your parents, your teachers, your workmates or your neighbours might see them is agonising and humiliating. Yet it can be very difficult to get action from social media or other websites where these images have been posted.

In the 1990s, the idea that we might one day have a significant social problem with image-based abuse would have been incomprehensible. But since then there have been several big changes. The first is that most of us now carry a smartphone, a device equipped to take high-resolution photographs and videos, along with audio. The second big change is that smartphones are connected to the internet—the images or videos we capture on them can be uploaded instantly. In turn, that means the image or video can be viewed, instantly, by a virtually unlimited number of people.

These two developments are technological in nature, but there has also been an important economic change. It used to be expensive to take (or at least to develop) photos. It also used to be expensive to make additional copies of photos. But with today's digital technology, and due to the business models under which that technology is provided to consumers, it typically costs nothing to take or share an image.

There has also been a major change in social behaviour. It is now commonplace in relationships to take and exchange intimate photographs. Unfortunately, relationships end, and some end badly. Sometimes an unhappy party may choose to post an intimate image of their former partner online. In some cases the images are authentic, albeit originally intended only for an intimate partner, not for wide dissemination. In other cases the images are fake, having been manipulated using sophisticated technology that makes them look real. Either way, the impact on the victim is devastating.

Image-based abuse is unfortunately just one example of the many kinds of harmful or undesirable content that can be widely distributed over the internet. In a world where nearly five billion people are online and have the capacity to create and post content, some of that content is going to be harmful or threatening or offensive. So why exactly is this a big new problem? And what can governments do about it?

The Big New Problem

Traditionally, governments have made rules about what appears in books, magazines and newspapers, and over the past century such rules have been extended to radio, movies and television. The regulation of content occurs for many reasons. Classification schemes—in Australia, for example, movies are rated on a scale extending from G to PG, M, MA, R and X— were originally justified on moral grounds, to limit depictions of nudity, sex or violence. More recently, the justification has been to provide consumer information, particularly for parents, so their children are not exposed to age-inappropriate content.

There have always been categories of content that have been subject to regulation. There are limits on what you can say in criticising other people, under the law of defamation. There are restrictions on publishing information about how to make a bomb or a chemical weapon, or how to commit suicide, for public safety reasons. There are constraints on publicising the activities of the armed forces or intelligence agencies, for national security reasons. And under intellectual property laws, if the rights to particular content, such as copyright in a book, are owned by somebody else, you cannot publish that content without the owner's consent, usually linked to a payment arrangement.

Furthermore, historically it was reasonably straight-forward to enforce these restrictions, because very few people could afford to publish or distribute an image or a piece of text so that it could be seen by more than a handful of people. Only a small number of enterprises had the capacity to disseminate content broadly. These were, in the main, professional media businesses, and they exercised tight editorial control over their platforms. For this reason, the vast bulk of the kind of material we consider harmful online today never made it near their screens or pages.

For governments, this was convenient. To regulate or control content, you only needed to deal with a handful of organisations that were generally well resourced, incentivised to behave lawfully, and, in the main, operating only within your own borders. By engaging with a small number of book and newspaper publishers, television networks and radio stations, a government could pretty much cover the field.

In the last thirty years, these certainties have been swept away by the internet. The task for a government now wishing to regulate the content its citizens can access has fundamentally changed. People all over the world are posting content that can be seen by your citizens, be it on Facebook, Twitter, LinkedIn or Instagram, or on websites based in countries where the rule of law is weak. Both varieties have created fresh problems for governments that wish to continue their traditional role of protecting citizens by regulating content.

Some argue that these developments are wholly positive. No longer can repressive regimes control the flow of information to citizens, they say. The yoke of censorship has been lifted, and adults are free to view whatever content suits their tastes. I think such arguments are, at best, naive. When it comes to the internet and autocratic governments, controls are still very effectively enforced. A good example is the Chinese Government's restrictions on Western social media platforms, and its close monitoring of what is posted on Chinese platforms such as WeChat.

What these arguments also overlook is the work of government in protecting public order and safety. And the internet creates significant new challenges for this work. People have always been able to make statements that are personally abusive, that are designed to dupe or mislead those who read them, or that provide instructions about how to build a weapon or hijack an aircraft or otherwise hurt yourself or others. But today, such a statement made online—at zero cost to the person making it—can be visible to potentially many, many people. In other words, these harms have always been possible, but the internet greatly magnifies their reach.

We can joke about emails offering us the chance to receive millions of dollars from the Nigerian Central Bank, if only we will provide all of our bank account details, including our passwords, but the sad fact is that Australians regularly lose money to online scams. According to the ACCC, Australians lost more than $634 million to such scams in 2019.[16] More sinister still are the devastating crimes where people, including young children, are induced to perform sexual acts over a webcam and then blackmailed: 'Pay us $10 000 and no-one needs to see this video, otherwise it will be seen by everybody you know'. Similarly, being a victim of ransomware is devastating to businesses: software is inadvertently downloaded to your computer, it causes your vital business records to be locked, and it is soon followed by a demand that you pay a substantial sum of money to have the records unlocked.

If governments cannot protect their citizens from such crimes, public confidence will rapidly fall. Taken a step further, imagine the impact on public confidence and order if power, phone, or water and sewerage systems stopped working. In a world where such systems are controlled by networked computers, there is an ever-present risk that those computers could have malicious software loaded onto them, allowing a hostile foreign power or criminals to take control of the services that underpin modern life.

In the late twentieth century, terrorists wishing to disrupt the Australian economy might have chosen to do so by bombing a key power plant—today, the same outcome might be achieved by using the internet to install malicious code on the computers controlling that power plant.

The internet, then, offers new ways in which long-known harms can be carried out. Even worse, it can bring entirely new harms. Consider the appalling Christchurch mosque attacks in March 2019. Fifty-one people were murdered. Horrifyingly, the killings were live-streamed on Facebook, meaning the impact of the violence was not limited to the victims and the immediate witnesses but disseminated to an enormous audience of viewers across the world. This simply could not have happened a few years ago when the bandwidth on mobile networks was not sufficient and sophisticated live-streaming applications did not exist.

For decades, we have had rules about the kind of content people can be shown on television. There are carefully designed codes about what may be broadcast at particular times, including, for example, whether violence may be shown and at what level of intensity. The idea that live footage of people being murdered could be made available to a viewing audience around the globe would have been beyond the comprehension of citizens and governments when the laws that regulate free-to-air television were devised.

What Can Governments Do?

In 2011, I was a recently arrived Liberal MP in Canberra. Having worked in the telecommunications industry, I was writing and speaking about the public policy issues posed by the internet. One day, then Opposition leader Tony Abbott called me to ask if I would lead a working group of Coalition MPs in looking at how we could help keep young people safe when accessing the internet. My colleagues and I plunged into this work, visiting schools around the country and speaking with experts on the emerging issues of cyberbullying and online safety. We developed a detailed policy, including a promise to establish a new government office—a Children's eSafety Commissioner.

By 2013 we were in government and I had been appointed parliamentary secretary to the then minister for communications, Malcolm Turnbull, with one of my jobs being to turn our election policy into law. I recall joining Malcolm on a visit to Silicon Valley in early 2014, where we met senior executives at Facebook, Google and other big tech companies. In one discussion, Malcolm asked a senior executive for his views on cyberbullying: was any kind of government intervention needed to curtail the problem and lessen the damage being done to our kids? I can still vividly remember the executive's response. He leaned back in his chair, placed his hands behind his head, and said expansively, 'You know, minister, we are doing an awesome job on these issues'.

There was clearly a very big gulf between the view of the world from Silicon Valley and the perspective we had gained from parents and schoolchildren as we travelled around Australia. The latter had told us that if you were the victim of cyberbullying, it was impossible to get the platforms in question to take the material down. Indeed, it was often impossible even to lodge a complaint—certainly you had no chance of speaking to a human being. And if you went to the police, while they were usually sympathetic, they did not know what to do either—and they had a lot of other pressing problems to deal with.

Back in Australia, we introduced legislation to establish the Children's eSafety Commissioner as well as a cyberbullying take-down scheme to deal with damaging online content targeted at young Australians—to date, more than 2500 Australian children have been assisted by this scheme. We have since expanded the office to support all Australians— it is now simply the eSafety Commissioner—and given it new powers. Thanks in part to Noelle Martin's advocacy, we passed laws in 2018 to give the commissioner the ability to require a website to take down unauthorised intimate images, which has since led to nearly 4000 complaints of image-based abuse being lodged.[17]

Following the 2019 Christchurch mosque attacks, Prime Minister Scott Morrison successfully pushed at the G20 for joint action to force social media companies to do more to remove terrorist and other extremist content from their platforms. Meanwhile, in Australia, we gave the eSafety Commissioner regulatory powers over a new category of harm: 'abhorrent violent material'. In addition, as I write this, the parliament has just passed a new *Online Safety Act* designed to further build the eSafety Commissioner's powers and resources, including the ability to order the removal of serious cyber-abuse directed at an Australian adult—an extension of the cyberbullying scheme, but with a higher threshold, recognising that adults are more resilient than children.

I do not claim for an instant that we have all the solutions to the regulation of online content. In fact, there is plenty of work ahead for the Australian Government, as there is for other governments around the world. Much remains to be done in three areas in particular.

The first is defamation. There have long been restrictions on what you can say about another person in a publication or another publicly accessible medium. If you say something negative about somebody, that person can sue you. If the court finds you have caused serious harm to that person's reputation, you can be liable to pay damages. But exactly how the law of defamation should deal with comments posted online is a matter that remains unsettled. One practical problem is that the internet, and the social media platforms operating through it, have made it possible for vastly larger numbers of people to comment on others, and to have those comments seen, potentially, by a huge audience. As a result, the sheer volume of possible defamation cases is much greater than it was before the internet was widely accessed.

Then there is the question of who is responsible for the comment. If an article in *The Sydney Morning Herald* is unfairly critical of me, I can sue the publisher of that newspaper. That makes sense: a newspaper carefully curates and edits its content. But the business model of a social media platform like Facebook does not involve the diligent curating or editing of content. It is for this reason that internet businesses have long argued that they should not be liable for the content posted on their sites.

In many ways, it is surprising this position has been quite widely accepted by courts and governments around the world. Imagine if I owned 200 billboards in prominent sites around Sydney, and I invited people to submit to me statements about other people which I then put up on those billboards, statements that contained nasty and factually incorrect claims. If the subjects of those claims complained to me, or sought to sue me for defamation, I would likely not get much public sympathy if I said, 'I am not responsible. My business model does not include vetting the accuracy of the statements which I put up on my billboards'. Yet this is effectively what the digital platforms have been saying.

In Australia, defamation law is the responsibility of state and territory governments, not the federal government. In June 2021, NSW Attorney-General Mark Speakman, on behalf of all state and territory attorneys-general, put out a thoughtful discussion paper about this very issue. It specifically considers the question of whether a digital platform like Facebook, Twitter or LinkedIn should be liable under defamation law for statements made on it. The discussion paper suggests that

[t]here are a number of potential policy grounds for a range of internet intermediaries having some

responsibility in defamation law for the publication of third-party content where they have created systems or online environments to enable and promote the publication and dissemination of user-generated content.[18]

A second area that needs attention is the problem of misinformation on social media. Are 5G mobile networks harmful? Are vaccines dangerous? Will drinking unpasteurised milk protect you against cancer? Today, there is nothing to stop complete nonsense being posted online. Unlike traditional media businesses, social media platforms do not curate or edit or fact-check what is posted. The problem would be serious enough if it were simply the result of foolish or ill-informed people posting inaccurate statements on areas in which they do not have subject-matter expertise. But it is worse when this is done with deliberate intent. (In the jargon, the first kind of content is called 'misinformation'; when it is done with intent, it is 'disinformation'.) For example, hostile foreign governments are suspected to have posted false information on social media to seek to influence recent US presidential elections. This was done in industrial quantities using technologies such as automated 'bots'.

Some people question whether this can or should be dealt with by social media platforms, by identifying such material and blocking it on the basis that it violates their terms of use. The issue came into sharp focus when Twitter suspended the account of then US president Donald Trump in early January 2021, with his supporters criticising this as an attack on free speech. Of course, there has never been an absolute right to free speech. In the classic legal formulation, nobody is free to shout 'Fire!' in a crowded theatre. Nor is there anything new in private corporations deciding who is able to say what on their platforms. Traditional media outlets such as television and radio stations and newspapers routinely impose restrictions on what people are able to say.

In Australia, we have followed a model adopted by the European Union on this issue. In February 2021, our media regulator, the Australian Communications and Media Authority, registered a voluntary Code of Practice on Misinformation and Disinformation that was developed by the digital industry.[19] Industry participants have committed to comply with the requirements of this code, though only time will tell if this is sufficient to deal with the issue, or whether more direct regulation will be needed.

A third area where more work is needed is age-appropriate content. Historically, enforcing content requirements was relatively straightforward. The only way to see a movie was in a cinema; if you could not prove at the box office that you were eighteen or older, then you were not going to see a movie that was rated 'R'. Today, however, most children carry smartphones or tablets or laptops, and it is no coincidence that about a quarter of Australian parents of kids aged six to seventeen have told the eSafety Commissioner they think their children have been, or are likely to have been, exposed to online porn— of those, 40 per cent said their child came across it accidentally.[20]

This is a vexing issue. Many parents are troubled by the kind of adult content children can be exposed to online. Regularly, I hear people argue that technology is the answer; for example, making filters mandatory. In my view, technology is certainly part of the solution—Apple and Android smartphones come with parental control tools, and there are filters that work quite effectively to block adult content. But merely making the technology available is not enough. The problem is that many parents are unsure of how to use these tools; some are not even aware they exist.

The new *Online Safety Act 2021* will give the regulator new powers to require that providers of smartphones take reasonable steps to protect children from exposure to this type of material, with tools such as age-assurance mechanisms and child safety risk assessments. We want to make these types of features the default, so parents know when they buy a device marketed as child-suitable that it has controls in place.

Recently, an Australian parliamentary committee has been looking at these issues. It has called for laws mandating that websites offering adult content must have a 'restricted access system'; that is, when you visit these sites, you must prove you are at least eighteen years old before you can see any of the content. In response, the federal government has asked the eSafety Commissioner to develop a road map concerning the required technology. As part of that work, it will be important to look at previous attempts in this area, including a major program in Britain which fell over just before the December 2019 UK election. But whatever the solution ends up being, this is clearly an area where more work is needed.

The range of content available online is extraordinary. Much of it is of considerable social value. Some of it is junk. Some of it is harmful. When people go online, there are benefits to be gained—but there are also risks. That means plenty of work for government in its traditional role as a content regulator.

BUSINESSES AND CONSUMERS

For many decades, Australians took for granted some realities about how the taxi industry worked. You could forget about getting a taxi at 'changeover time', around three o'clock in the afternoon. You could expect to wait a very long time for a taxi on a Saturday night—when you did manage to get one, it was sometimes smelly or badly maintained. And if the trip you wanted to take was not long enough, or going in the wrong direction for the driver's taste, the driver might refuse to take you. In fairness to the drivers, they often faced poor behaviour from passengers. But their biggest problem was they were not making much money: a good deal of what they earned went to the owner of the taxi licence.

It was hardly surprising, then, that when Uber came along, Australians took to it enthusiastically. You could order a ride on your smartphone, know exactly how long you would wait (and watch a little map showing the vehicle getting closer to you), pay conveniently without having to use cash or get your credit card out, and rate the driver (and be rated) as a means of encouraging a courteous interaction on both sides. Uber is a textbook example of the way the internet has disrupted industry after industry. The combination of the internet and smartphones allowed a new business model for individualised public transport. For the consumer, it was a vastly better service and people flocked to use it. For people wanting to earn some extra money by driving their own vehicle for Uber, it was attractive.

But the holders of the taxi licences were predictably unhappy because the value of their licences fell sharply. And they had paid a lot of money for them—in New South Wales, several hundred thousand dollars was the typical price paid for one of the 6000 taxi licences on issue. The high prices reflected government limits on the number of licences, but while these suited the industry, they did not serve consumers well at all. Unsurprisingly, governments soon came under considerable political pressure from the taxi industry. In New South Wales, the government responded with a $250 million compensation scheme for taxi licence-holders, funding it via a $1 levy on every ride in a taxi or Uber.

The story is similar for many other Australian businesses that have been disrupted by the internet—from newspapers to street directories to encyclopedias to video stores—although few have succeeded in being compensated as the taxi industry has been. Still, it is far too simplistic to say the internet has been bad for the national economy in general, and Australian businesses specifically. Certainly, many have been destroyed by the internet. But numerous new businesses have been created by Australian entrepreneurs, or existing ones have been restructured, to take advantage of the possibilities the internet has opened up. And for Australian consumers, the internet has been an overwhelmingly positive development.

Bad News for Many Businesses

The internet has brought successive waves of disruption. An early wave completely up-ended the newspaper business. Classified advertisements were famously referred to as the 'rivers of gold' that made newspaper businesses extremely valuable in Australia. Papers like *The Sydney Morning Herald*, the *Daily Telegraph*, *The Age* and the *Courier Mail* put their owners—the Fairfaxes, the Packers and the Murdochs—among the wealthiest families in Australia. But today, if you want to buy or sell a house or a car, find a job or hire an employee, specialist websites deliver better results for both the advertiser and the potential buyer than a print advertisement. Over the past thirty years, businesses like Domain, realestate.com.au, Drive, carsales.com.au and Seek have become highly profitable, while over the same period, newspaper classified advertising revenues have fallen by 90 per cent.

Another wave of disruption came with the smartphone. Apple released the iPhone in 2007, meaning consumers could now access the internet pretty much wherever they were. The future of printed street directories—*Melways*, *Gregorys* and others—became very bleak, very quickly. It was much more convenient to find your destination using Google Maps or Apple Maps on your smartphone, a device that could even give you spoken directions as you drove, something no paper-based directory could match.

In the years that followed, the typical fixed-line internet speeds available to consumers began to rise sharply. In 2010, only about a third of Australian households could get 8 Mbps or more.[21] Today, about 70 per cent of the NBN's almost eight million customers are on a plan that is 50 Mbps or higher.[22] The wide availability of high-speed broadband sparked further change, typically based on video content. YouTube quickly built a big global position as a platform for user-uploaded video. Meanwhile, Netflix, which had started out in the late 1990s by sending DVDs through the mail in response to orders lodged online, developed a new business category: the streaming-video-on-demand platform. When this service launched in Australia in 2015, Australians responded enthusiastically—for a pricepoint of around $10 a month, they could access an enormous catalogue of movies and TV shows. Within two months of its launch, more than one million Australians across 400 000 households had signed up to Netflix.[23]

In an extremely disruptive move by Netflix, it began to commission high-budget, high-production-value, made-for-Netflix television shows, miniseries and movies. Before long, Netflix originals like *House of Cards* were attracting huge global audiences. No longer was a 'straight to video' movie seen as playing in the second division of screening compared with a cinematic release. A Netflix-commissioned movie typically has a budget almost as big as a movie made for theatrical release, and big-name movie stars generally have been happy to appear in such movies.

The impact on broadcast television has been profound. Typical evening prime-time audiences on combined metropolitan free-to-air television networks in Australia fell from 3.6 million in 2010 to 2.6 million by 2019.[24] Their loss has been the streaming video providers' gain—today, 70 per cent of Australian households have at least one streaming-video-on-demand service.[25]

Good News for Australian Consumers

For every business that is disrupted, however, there is a flip side—an internet-based business that provides consumers with a new service, or an existing service done better, or an existing service provided more cheaply. And Australians have determinedly taken up these new offerings.

Consider how the internet and digital technology make it so much easier to book, pay for and use an airline ticket. No longer do you have to make a booking in the office of a travel agent, either by telephone or going there physically. The days of paper-based tickets, which could take days to be processed, are long gone, along with the stress of keeping them safe for the whole trip. Today, on a website like Expedia or Webjet, you can use the internet to find out within a few seconds what flights are available, at what time and at what cost. To make and pay for a booking are near-instantaneous acts. You can book flights and hotels online from any device, anywhere, anytime, and have confirmation arrive via email. Increasingly, the entire process is paperless, with the ticket and then the boarding pass sent to your smartphone, making them virtually impossible to lose.

The service experience today, compared with that offered twenty-five years ago, has improved phenomenally, whether we're talking about travel, banking, buying books or clothes or music, or searching for a house or car to buy. If you want to buy a house, for example, searching on a website like Domain.com.au is quicker, easier and more informative than reading through a series of classified ads. Similarly, looking online for a car is much more efficient than traipsing from car dealer to car dealer.

In many instances, the internet lets consumers do things that were unimaginable even twenty years ago. For people who like music, for example, the internet has completely changed what they can do. In the 1950s, 1970s or even 1990s, music lovers would painstakingly build up collections of records—later, compact discs—of their favourite bands or singers. To choose whom you wanted to listen to required working through a physical pile of records, probably stacked on a shelf. If they got damaged, too bad: no more music. If you had the Beatles' first album, you could listen to the fourteen tunes it contained, but if you wanted to listen to any of their other tunes, you had to go to a shop and buy another album. To own all of the albums issued by just one band was a very expensive exercise, probably costing a consumer several hundred dollars.

The idea that you could pay a modest monthly subscription allowing you, whenever you chose, to listen to any of the songs ever issued by any one of many thousands of bands and individual artists would have seemed an impossible fantasy a few decades ago. Today, Spotify and many other music services have made that possible—and if you do not want to pay for a subscription, you can choose an advertising-funded version of the service instead. You do not need a separate music collection in your home, or in your car, or at work—one collection is accessible just about anywhere, over any internet-connected device.

The largest single cost in many household budgets across Australia is the monthly mortgage payment. It used to be that comparing interest rates was a painstaking process. You had to ring around all the banks to get the information you needed—whether you were a new buyer or an existing homeowner considering whether you should shift to another financial institution. Today, you can go to a comparison website like Canstar and in under a minute get an accurate, industry-wide comparison of all the different rates available. Then, with the click of a mouse, you can connect to the website of the bank offering the most attractive rate and fill out an online application form. Such a search could very easily help you reduce your interest rate from, say, 3 per cent to 2.5 per cent— an annual saving of around $2000 for a mortgage of $400 000.[26]

Economists continue to get excited about the way the internet has allowed consumers to be much better informed about the prices on offer in the marketplace. In the pre-internet world, it took time, effort and money—'search costs' in the economic jargon—to gather such information. Many consumers did not bother and as a result paid higher prices. But now that information is much more easily and cheaply available. Again in econospeak, the internet has greatly reduced the 'information asymmetry' between the businesses selling goods and services, and the consumers buying them.

There is a further reason why the internet has brought such big benefits to consumers: you now have a bigger choice of merchants from whom to buy. That is a benefit for consumers everywhere, but it is arguably biggest in small and distant markets like Australia, as opposed to big and established markets such as those in the United States and Europe.

Think about how buying clothes in Australia has changed. In the pre-internet days, Australians put up with poor-quality clothing sold at high prices. Because we are a small market, manufacturers could not justify giving us the extent of choice available in the much bigger national markets. I still remember travelling to the United States as a student in the 1980s and being amazed at how, in the big-chain clothing stores, you had a choice of not just waist size but also length when buying trousers. In similar shops in Australia, you chose your waist size and you got whatever length the manufacturer deemed appropriate—if it was too long, you could get it taken up; if it was too short, tough.

Australians used to put up with higher prices for books and wait months to read them after they were first released in London and New York. A cosy global cartel of book publishers relegated the Australian market to well down the priority list. Today, with the option of ordering hard-copy books on sites like Amazon or Booktopia, or having a soft copy delivered instantly to a computer or Kindle or other device, things are quite different.

I have taken the time to emphasise the sundry consumer benefits the internet has brought because they are significant and they are very real economic effects. Another bit of jargon used by economists is 'consumer surplus', which can be crudely defined as the dollar value of the benefits consumers get when they purchase something they value but pay less for it than they would actually be willing to pay. The internet has delivered enormous consumer surplus because in so many areas, consumers, in Australia and across the world, are getting better services at lower prices than they were paying even just a few years ago.

What about the Production Side?

Some say Australia is living in a fool's paradise: we are consuming madly over the internet, but we're not producing anything online, so our long-term economic prospects are therefore grim. Australians certainly are great consumers of products and services over the internet, and much of what we buy is generated in other countries. And the giant online platforms through which Australians typically acquire goods or services—from Amazon to eBay, Facebook, Google, Uber, Airbnb, Expedia and Netflix—are typically foreign owned. So shouldn't we be worried, then, about how the internet is becoming an ever more dominant part of the global economy, and yet Australians are doing much less selling online than buying? Isn't there a risk that, as the global economy continues its transformation, our prosperity will decline because Australia does not have a strong presence on the production side of the internet?

These concerns are regularly raised by people working in the technology sector. For example, Alan Noble, an Australian who worked for Google in Silicon Valley for many years before returning to Australia, put the issue this way in an article he wrote in 2012: 'Australia risks remaining the consumers, rather than becoming the creators, of technology. This is the difference between *using* a smartphone and *creating* an app that reaches millions of people'.[27] In 2014, Australian technology billionaire and Atlassian co-founder Mike Cannon-Brookes had this to say:

> Technology is going to be the major driver of change over the next twenty-five years. It has been over the

last twenty-five. Now, if we're not participating as a country in creating that technology, we're going to be purely a consumer of overseas technology. We're not going to have the wealth created here …[28]

Noble and Cannon-Brookes both have extremely impressive track records in the technology sector. What they say needs to be taken seriously. Yet, when I hear comments like this, I cannot help but reflect on earlier stages of the debate in Australia about technology and whether we are falling behind in this area.

In the mid-1990s, a commonplace call was that Australia needed to have its own 'fab plant' (a factory for fabricating semiconductors). We needed to manufacture silicon chips in Australia—if we did not, then we faced becoming economically marginalised. However, as history now records, Australia stuck with its traditional industries and enjoyed the fruits of a massive commodities boom. Indeed, by 2013, the Credit Suisse World Wealth Report would rank Australia second-highest on average household wealth, and highest on median household wealth, of all the nations in the world.

I certainly do not contest the proposition there were profound digital transformations underway in the 1990s, and nearly thirty years on they are continuing at an even greater pace. On the contrary, I strongly believe that digital disruption is one of the most fundamental forces affecting our economy. In their book, *Why Nations Fail: The Origins of Power, Prosperity and Poverty*, US economists Daron Acemoglu and James A Robinson argue that 'during the critical juncture created by the Industrial Revolution, many nations missed the boat and failed to take advantage of the spread of industry'.[29] Today, the economic transformation being driven by the internet and digital technology is in many ways comparable to the Industrial Revolution (although, as I discussed earlier, US economist Robert J Gordon argues that the Industrial Revolution had an even bigger economic impact than the internet). But, however you measure it, the internet is transforming economies, so it is natural to worry about whether we are missing the boat in our response.

What then, should Australia be doing to respond to this global economic transformation?

Capturing the Economic Opportunities

I think there are three important things to keep in mind when considering how to make the most of the economic opportunities at hand.

First, although the internet is becoming an

ever-bigger part of the global economy, we need to remember it is not the whole global economy. There are other segments that are big and important, and some of those are powerhouses of the Australian economy, such as agriculture and resources. For example, iron ore generated $117 billion in export earnings for Australia in 2020, natural gas $36 billion and coal $43 billion.[30] In more normal years—years not spent grappling with a pandemic—education and tourism would also be big export earners.

In 2010, then Reserve Bank governor Glenn Stevens gave a fascinating example of this. He pointed out that over the previous five years, the change in relative prices of iron ore and digital devices had given us the power to buy a lot more devices. In 2005, one shipload of iron ore from Australia was worth 2200 imported flat-screen TVs, but by 2010 it was worth 22 000 flat-screen TVs.[31]

I am not arguing we should ignore the internet because we can make our money in other ways. Rather, I am pointing out that we want an Australian economy that has strengths across many sectors. We should celebrate and build on our traditional areas of strength like agriculture, resources and financial services, and at the same time build many more businesses, particularly larger ones, in the fast-growing technology and internet sector.

Second, we need to acknowledge that the internet has made the world a more intensively competitive place. On the plus side, this means that, despite being a long way from the major markets, Australia has the capacity to be globally competitive in developing and exporting a product such as software. Atlassian, for one, is a world leader in software that allows development teams to communicate with each other and manage their workflows. Founded in 2002 by two young University of New South Wales engineering graduates, Mike Cannon-Brookes and Scott Farquhar, it has grown remarkably and today its annualised revenue stands at US$2 billion.

Consider, too, the profitable business of making animated movies. It requires high-powered computers and sophisticated software; it also requires traditional skills such as crafting and telling a good story. All of which Australia has. We are home to world-leading businesses like Animal Logic, the producer of blockbuster movies like *Peter Rabbit* (grossed more than US$350 million worldwide) and *Happy Feet* (more than US$384 million).[32] Adelaide's Rising Sun Pictures was nominated for an Oscar for its work on *X-Men: Days of Future Past*.[33]

On the negative side, businesses located in lots of other countries can also be world-competitive. So in the internet era, it is more important than ever to work out what your strengths are—and where you are going to be good enough to build not just a strong market share in Australia but a strong market share globally. Australia has a world-class, large-scale resources industry; so, too, is our agriculture world-class. So it makes sense that the development of IT applications and services to make these industries more productive and efficient is a niche in which Australian companies have an advantage.

Australia is already a global leader in R&D for mining automation. Some years ago, I had the chance to visit the extremely impressive Rio Tinto Control Centre in Perth. Some 300 people work in this centre, which controls fourteen mines, multiple railway lines and several ports, all 1500 kilometres away in the Pilbara. It is a powerful demonstration of how modern mining is extremely capital-intensive, highly technologically sophisticated, and just as susceptible to productivity improvement through digital technology as is banking, travel, entertainment or any other industry.

There are similar opportunities to develop world-leading technology to support the Australian agricultural sector. Applying digital technologies, such as low-cost sensors, can assist farmers in monitoring irrigation, soil moisture, vegetation, livestock and farm equipment. I recently visited Adelaide-based technology company Myriota, which has launched a network of low-Earth-orbiting satellites that cover the entire planet. Founder Alex Grant explained how the company specialises in small, low-cost satellites which gather relatively small amounts of data, but can do it very cheaply and efficiently, and from any location on Earth. A key market for Myriota is farmers who need to see the data gathered on devices like soil moisture monitors and rainfall gauges.

Alex showed me a rainfall gauge made by Australian company Goanna Ag—it is designed to sit on a star-shaped fence post—and a small piece of electronics made by Myriota which allows the gauge to be networked. The data is transferred to a satellite whenever it passes overhead (typically two or three times a day), and it is then sent to a ground station and fed into sophisticated software. The output of that software is a web-based tool which farmers can access by logging in online, to gain a comprehensive picture of rainfall levels on a farm. As Alex pointed out to me, because of Australia's large distances and low population density, Myriota has a particular focus on these kinds of problems. But there is a global market: plenty of customers in other countries face similar problems and are interested in using the company's services.

This brings me to my third point: what should the Australian Government be doing to support businesses in finding productive niches in the new global economy? It should not mean bureaucrats in Canberra try to decide where those market niches are; that job is best done by the private sector. But there are important 'enablers' for business activity that should be a focus for government.

One such enabler is an Australia-wide, high-speed digital network, so businesses can connect to that network and thereby the world wherever in Australia they are located. The Australian Government has invested nearly $50 billion in the NBN. There are around twelve million premises in Australia—all but a handful can now connect to the NBN if they choose, and over eight million premises now are connected.

Another enabler is having a strong venture-capital sector which is able to fund technology start-ups to grow to their next stage. Over the last ten years, this sector has expanded considerably in Australia. Home-grown tech success stories include companies like Atlassian (collaboration tools), Afterpay (retail fintech), Canva (graphic design platform), Airwallex (cross-border payments), Campaign Monitor (marketing), Brighte (fintech/home improvement) and 3P Learning (education software).

Yet another enabler is national policy settings that create a demand for digital solutions. Two good examples are Australia's national system of digital health records, and the work our government is doing to set up a national digital identity system.

It is also worth noting one key enabler of the digital economy in Australia which has little to do with government and everything to do with the behaviours of Australians themselves. Australian consumers are enthusiastic early adopters of technology. The take-up of payWave technology is a good example: in 2019, 83 per cent of point-of-sale transactions in Australia were contactless, initiated by tapping a debit or credit card, including 5 per cent by a mobile device (such as a smartphone or other payment-enabled device, like a watch).[34]

There is plenty of negative commentary about Australia's economy not being sufficiently digitally enabled. Some compare us to the United States or China—in both cases an unfair comparison given they are enormous markets able to support massive consumer businesses like Facebook or Tencent, which can build a domestic customer base of hundreds of millions before they take their first step out into the world.

I first began working in this policy space in 1996, when I joined the staff of then minister for communications Richard Alston. Over the past twenty-five years, I have visited a lot of incubators and start-ups and technology businesses, in Australia and internationally—from Israel to Sweden, to the United States, New Zealand, Malaysia, Singapore and many other countries. I have worked with a lot of people in technology, including during the eight years I spent on the senior management team of Optus. And I have been involved in plenty of public policy work on the question of how best to maximise Australia's economic performance in the internet age. Based on that experience, I have a more positive view than I see in much of the commentary. I believe Australia has an impressive track record of digital achievement, and an enormous digital potential that we are increasingly exercising.

Some compare Australia to Israel, undoubtedly a digital superpower with a presence much greater than its population of nine million would suggest. Others compare us to Estonia, a world leader in government use of IT, or to Singapore, which uses tax and policy levers to very aggressively court start-ups. All of this rightly reminds us that the world is an intensively competitive place, and the internet has only made it more so.

There is, in fact, significant evidence of Australia's performance as a digital economy. Consider the findings of the 2018 report 'Preparing for Disruption' by the research and analysis division of *The Economist*, which ranks eighty-two of the world's largest economies on their technological readiness. In the forecast period of 2018–22, it places Australia in the number-one spot ahead of Singapore and Sweden—up from third place for the 2013–17 period behind Finland and Sweden.[35]

The 2020 *AFR* Young Rich List, comprising people aged forty or under, in my view also tells a powerful story. A clear majority of those on the list have made their fortunes from internet-based businesses. Even ten years ago, they would have come mainly from the property sector, sport or entertainment.

There is more to do. But Australia's internet-based businesses are strong, growing, and generating prosperity.

PRINCIPLES FOR GOVERNMENTS IN THE INTERNET AGE

The internet has changed, and is still changing, everything—including for governments. How, then, should governments be responding? What does good government look like in the internet age?

As I argued at the start of this book, thirty years ago we did not know the answer to that question. At the outset, the internet gave no indication of becoming a mass-market consumer phenomenon—many of the implications of an internet-enabled world were not yet known, and governments were slow to recognise the internet's disruptive ability. But governments are now much more confident in how they govern in a world that has been transformed by the internet. We do not have all the answers, and the rate of change continues to be extraordinary, making it difficult to predict what the world will look like in ten, twenty or fifty years. Even so, we know a lot more about what the internet means for society in general than we did in the 1990s. I think we can identify some key principles to guide governments in the internet age.

Paradoxically, a common theme is that what defined good government in the pre-internet age now applies even more intensely. For example, Australia remains a 'small open economy'; that is, we are a trading nation, we buy and sell in world markets, and if we are less productive and efficient than other countries, what we have to sell will earn less and in turn our national prosperity will decline. The internet only makes these forces operate more intensely. It is harder, not easier, to try to protect ourselves behind high-tariff walls in an internet-enabled world. Such a protectionist approach was folly in the 1960s and 1970s, leading to our eventual repudiation of it in the 1980s. It would be even more foolish to attempt this in a world where consumers can purchase goods and services online in a global marketplace.

Accept Greater Transparency, Scrutiny and Visibility

In the internet age, every institution in our society—including government—faces much more visibility and scrutiny than before.

In December 2010, the so-called Arab Spring began with a street vendor in Tunisia setting himself alight as a protest against a corrupt government. The act sparked a popular movement that quickly spread to other Arab nations, including Libya, Bahrain and Egypt. Activists used social media to share information, organise protests and other activities, and publicise their efforts globally. As one Egyptian activist tweeted: 'We use Facebook to schedule the protests, Twitter to coordinate, and YouTube to tell the world'.[36]

Social media channels worked to share political content during the Arab Spring. In the week prior to Egyptian president Hosni Mubarak's resignation, for example, the number of tweets about political change increased exponentially—from 2300 a day to 230 000 a day.[37] There was plenty of talk about 'Twitter revolutions' and the role of the internet as a force for social change. Then president of the Internet Society in Tunisia, Khaled Koubaa, explained how 'social media was absolutely critical' to the Arab Spring movement:

Three months before Mohammed Bouazizi burned himself in Sidi Bouzid we had a similar case in Monastir. But no one knew about it because it was not filmed. What made a difference this time is that the images of Bouazizi were put on Facebook and everybody saw it.[38]

Sadly, as it turned out, much of the commentary of the time proved to be overblown. In Egypt, the Mubarak regime was overthrown—only to be replaced within days by a new military administration. The simplistic claim that a corrupt or oppressive regime could not survive an internet-organised campaign proved to be wrong. But what was highlighted was that the internet exposes governments—whether authoritarian or democratic—to much greater transparency, visibility and scrutiny.

Regularly, there are instances of government officials—soldiers, police and others—captured in photos or videos harassing or intimidating or brutalising people. Footage taken by witnesses of the 2020 arrest by police in Minneapolis of George Floyd, which resulted in his death by suffocation—arresting officer Derek Chauvin knelt on Floyd's neck for over nine minutes—sparked huge protests across the United States and internationally. Prior to the existence of the internet, such an episode would have been very difficult to record. It would have been even more difficult for the recording to be widely distributed. Today, however, such events can be made visible to very large numbers of people very quickly.

Such increased visibility is, in the main, a good thing rather than a bad one. The idea that we are all 'citizen journalists', equipped with a device which can record sound, pictures and videos and transmit them around the world, is an extraordinarily powerful one. Undoubtedly, it can be a check on abuses of power, on bullying, on the intimidation of the powerless. Yet it also has a dark side. What of the way the internet and social media inflames the public mood and prompts the rapid formation of online mobs, and sometimes physical mobs? Many decisions taken by governments offend or disadvantage at least some part of the population. Assembling on Twitter or Facebook, such a grouping of the disenchanted can appear very large—and can succeed in overturning a decision that in actual fact serves the overall interests of the community.

Prudent governments will recognise they now face greater scrutiny than ever before. They will train their agencies to be aware of this reality, and to respond better. They will also take advantage of the related tools to deliver greater visibility to citizens. Whether it is online reports of trains running on time, or of waiting times for the approval of development applications, or the population size of endangered species, governments can use the internet to show the work they are doing and what they are achieving. Rather than being surprised by scrutiny, governments can prepare for it and indeed provide information in response to that scrutiny; for example, by publishing online extensive data showing outcomes of interest to citizens.

Seize the Opportunity to Serve Citizens Better

The internet also gives governments some remarkable opportunities to serve their citizens better. To some extent, this means playing catch-up with what private-sector businesses—banks, airlines, insurance companies and many others—are doing.

We have all come to expect that we can instantaneously view our bank balance and our financial transactions, even those which occurred just seconds ago. We all expect to go online and find, quickly, all of the different flight options between two cities, and to book one with the click of a mouse. We also expect the airline will keep a record of all the flights we have booked and offer us rewards if we have used that airline consistently. Yet, all too often, our experience interacting with government is nowhere near as efficient as our experience interacting with private providers. We wait days or weeks for a response to a query. We are forced to attend an office in person to prove our identity or to sign a document. We provide all our personal details to the Australian Tax Office, but when we want to get a passport from the Department of Foreign Affairs and Trade, or when we want to re-register our cars or renew our licences, we have to provide the same information all over again.

Some countries are doing much better on this front than others, earning a reputation for delivering internet-based services to their citizens in a way that reduces costs and waiting times—and at the same time increases confidence, convenience and certainty. The small European nation of Estonia is one. In 2001, Estonia became one of the first countries in the world to classify internet access as a human right. Today, 99 per cent of its public services are accessible online. This approach resulted in technology magazine *WIRED* naming Estonia 'the most advanced digital society in the world' in 2016.[39]

In recent years, other countries have been catching up, with Denmark and South Korea taking out first and second place, ahead of Estonia, in the United Nation's 2020 E-Government Survey. The survey examines the scope and quality of online services, the status of tele-communications infrastructure, and existing human capacity. Finland and Australia rounded out the top five of the 193 ranked member states.[40]

In Australia, federal and state/territory governments alike are taking the transition to digital government service very seriously. At the state level, the NSW Government is showing the way with Service NSW, which handles a whole range of services, licences and certificates—not only does it enable you to renew your driver's licence online, instead of having a physical licence, you can choose to have a digital licence which exists as an image on your smartphone.

The federal government, similarly, has established Services Australia. Again, the key aim is to allow people to interact online rather than needing to attend a government office in person. Through the Services Australia website, you can carry out many different transactions with different parts of government: pay tax, claim a Medicare refund, receive social security benefits and much else besides. None of this would be possible without the large-scale IT systems used by government, but another necessity is the universal capacity of citizens to access these systems, using the internet. This underpins a profound change in the way members of the community can deal with government.

Foster an Open, Globally Competitive Economy

For many decades, the Australian economy operated under a protectionist mindset. We had high-tariff walls, manufactured domestically, and actively discouraged Australians from buying directly from overseas. By the 1980s this model was no longer sustainable. The Hawke, Keating and Howard governments systematically opened up the economy, reducing tariffs and permitting new foreign-owned entrants in sectors like banking and telecommunications. The arrival of the internet then further linked the Australian economy to global trade in a way that was previously unimaginable. Australian consumers can now buy goods and services directly from suppliers around the world—whether it is streaming home entertainment through Netflix, ordering goods of all kinds through Amazon, or booking travel online through Tripadvisor.

This has proved the nail in the coffin of the old model of doing business in Australia, when manufacturers could give local consumers any old rubbish because they simply did not have the option to buy from overseas competitors. But what it also means is that, in just about every industry, Australian businesses are now competing in a global marketplace. If you cannot supply world-class goods or services, you will lose customers—that's the bad news. If you can supply world-class goods or services, the good news is the internet gives you the means to do so, to tap into a vastly bigger market.

One of the best-established principles of economics is that of comparative advantage. If two countries trade with each other, each one will do better if it concentrates on the thing it is better at doing. Australia is very good at extracting high-quality iron ore, while Japan does a better job of making steel. Both countries are better off, according to the theory of comparative advantage, if we focus on iron ore and Japan focuses on steel. In a world of internet-driven trade, this principle applies even more strongly than it did before. This means we need to have a clear idea of where Australian companies can be competitive: where do our strengths lie, and how can we play to those strengths?

We were not competitive making cars. Between 2003 and 2013, domestically made passenger cars as a proportion of total sales fell from 62 per cent to 30 per cent.[41] The inevitable result was a decision by overseas car companies to cease manufacturing in Australia. But we certainly have the capacity to be world-competitive in developing and exporting software—unlike many other products, because software is weightless and incurs no transport costs, we do not face a cost disadvantage from being a long way from major markets. As I argued earlier, it makes particular sense to focus on software and technology for sectors where Australia is internationally competitive, like agriculture and resources.

You Can and Should Regulate, But Not in the Same Way

What implications does the internet have regarding the capacity of governments to regulate—to make rules to keep citizens safe; provide for orderly and efficient interactions between individuals and businesses; collect taxes to fund the necessary expenditure on roads, schools and hospitals; and the myriad other responsibilities of governments in a modern mixed economy—as well as maintain a system of justice so those who have been wronged can seek some redress?

The internet has greatly changed many areas that governments have traditionally regulated. I wrote earlier about how it used to be much easier for governments to control access to particular kinds of content in line with community standards. That material might be explicit pornography; it might be instructions on how to build a bomb or create a biological weapon; it might be grossly racist or abusive material. What that material is will vary from era to era and society to society. The point is that giving effect to such community standards is a lot harder today when everybody has access to the internet. But harder— including the requirement for different regulatory tools—does not mean impossible.

It suits the interests of the giant corporations which have built enormously profitable businesses using the internet, to claim that any regulation of, or restriction on, what people can see is simply not possible technically. They say any restriction on the available content violates the principle of freedom of speech. These companies also argue that any limit placed on their activities by the government of any particular country risks condemning that country to being a technology backwater, cut off from economic progress. Ten or twenty years ago, such arguments were given more credence. Increasingly today, they are recognised for what they are: self-serving and inaccurate.

The fact is, governments of individual nations can regulate for what happens online within their own country or to their own citizens. I believe the work of our own eSafety Commissioner is a good example. Backed by the new *Online Safety Act* and a team of expert investigators, the commissioner will continue working to protect Australians against terrorist material, child sexual abuse material, cyber-abuse, image-based abuse and other forms of online harm.

There is more to do in this space, but it is completely wrong to claim such regulation is impossible.

Do Not Give up Your Sovereignty

Which brings me to another important principle when it comes to how governments should engage with the internet: do not give up your sovereignty. This principle has guided the Australian Government over the past three years as we have worked to deal with a serious public policy problem: global digital platforms like Google and Facebook have had so much market power in the Australian digital advertising market that advertising-funded news media businesses were at risk of becoming unsustainable. We dealt with this issue through a measured and orthodox public policy process.

In 2018, then treasurer Scott Morrison asked our competition regulator, the ACCC, to conduct a thorough investigation into the market power of Google and Facebook. The ACCC produced its 600-page report, containing twenty-three recommendations, in mid-2019. In December that year, the federal government announced it would take up almost all of the recommendations, including a 'news media bargaining code' governing the relationship between Google and Facebook on the one hand,

and Australian news media businesses on the other. The ACCC recommended this code regulate the way in which the two sets of parties dealt commercially in relation to content generated and paid for by the news media businesses. This content is used by the digital platforms to attract eyeballs to their sites—eyeballs they then very successfully monetise to generate enormous amounts of advertising revenue.

Following industry consultation, the ACCC produced a draft of the code in July 2020 and then sought feedback from all stakeholders, including the digital platforms. After further iterations and more consultation, draft legislation was introduced into the federal parliament in late 2020 and was considered by a Senate committee in January 2021. This was the point at which the global management teams of Google and Facebook began to pay serious attention to what was happening in a comparatively small market many thousands of kilometres away from their headquarters. Google threatened to shut down its services in Australia; Facebook briefly removed its news services. These were clear attempts to pressure the Australian Government into backing down.

But we held firm through multiple engagements and negotiations with both companies. Over a few weeks, I found myself participating in video conferences held with each of Google CEO Sundar Pichai,

Facebook's Mark Zuckerberg and Microsoft CEO Satya Nadella, meetings which were also attended by Prime Minister Morrison, Treasurer Frydenberg, or both. At one point, Treasurer Frydenberg personally negotiated over several days with Mark Zuckerberg. Labor and the cross-benchers supported the legislation; their resolve, like that of the government, only firmed in the face of the public threats from Google and Facebook.

As we stated both publicly and privately, our position was that the sovereign government of Australia would decide the laws that operate in Australia. We did not want either Google or Facebook to exit the Australian market, but if you do business here, you must comply with the laws made by our democratically elected parliament. New laws were passed by the parliament on 25 February 2021, and both Google and Facebook have since entered into commercial agreements with a considerable number of Australian news media businesses. In other words, the code is working as it was intended to do.

This was a highly visible example of the way large global internet businesses have sought to challenge Australia's sovereignty. They have done similar things in dealing with other nations. Google, for example, withdrew news products in Germany and it removed Google News from Spain, when those countries introduced rules designed to require payment to news media businesses when their content was accessed by digital platforms. And there have been many other indications of the attitude of the global tech businesses. I well remember meeting a US-based senior executive of Google when he was visiting Australia, quite early in my time as an MP. He stated what he considered an uncontested fact: company tax would soon be impossible to collect in a digital world. I did not agree with that claim then and I do not agree with it now. If you carry out economic activity as a business, you need to pay your fair share of tax—whether your business is online or offline makes no difference. As I write, Australia has just joined with other Organisation for Economic Co-operation and Development nations in committing to a new global approach to taxing multinational companies. The plan is designed to 'ensure a fairer distribution of profits and taxing rights among countries with regard to the largest multinational enterprises, including digital companies', according to the OECD.[42]

How, in practical terms, should the Australian Government, or any other government, assert its sovereignty against global internet businesses? In this industry, as in others, government needs to strike a balance between applying global standards and imposing its own laws locally. There are benefits in adopting international standards which should not be lightly dismissed. But as a sovereign government, Australia needs to retain the right to make laws which apply to what happens here.

Consider the global automotive market. The great majority of the 80–100 million new cars built around the world each year are made by a handful of giant automakers like Hyundai, Toyota and General Motors. They do so with an eye on global standards concerning many important matters, such as the safety of the vehicles, and the emission of dangerous gases such as oxides of nitrogen and sulphur. But each country also makes its own laws about the standards that vehicles sold in that country must meet. Australia's laws, created where we consider it justified, are set out in the *Road Vehicle Standards Act*. In the main, Australia adopts global standards in those laws, in turn meaning vehicles are cheaper and more accessible for Australian consumers. But we reserve the right to make our own laws where we consider it justified. A global car-maker is not permitted to import a car into Australia if it does not meet our legal requirements. The same principle should apply when it comes to the internet giants.

~

The internet has changed everything, for just about every human being, and certainly for every government. In turn, governments have needed to work out how to do things differently. It has not meant that governments have become irrelevant or powerless.

I believe the internet has made our world a better place. Of course, it has brought risks and challenges as well as opportunities. But so too did the arrival of new transportation technologies in the eighteenth and nineteenth centuries. Over time, we made laws to reduce the dangers introduced by cars and trains, and these technologies have brought immeasurable net benefits to humankind. I believe the same is true of the internet.

So my conclusion is an optimistic one. Identifying and managing the risks posed by the internet are absolutely within the wit and capacity of government. The focus for every government should be on how to take advantage of all the internet can do, to deliver better lives for citizens. All we know for certain is that the future will bring more waves of technology-driven change. I close by expressing my conviction that this change will continue to be a net positive—and a path to an even brighter future.

ACKNOWLEDGEMENTS

I first came into the communications sector in the mid-1990s, and in the twenty-five years since, I have been lucky to work with a lot of smart people. I thank them all (not just the small number I am able to name) for helping me to develop my thinking about this endlessly fascinating sector; some of that thinking is given form in this book.

Richard Alston, communications minister in the Howard government, was a fantastic and endlessly intellectually curious boss. I learned much from him and colleagues from that time, including David Quilty, the three Fionas (Cameron, Menzies and Poletti) and Neville Stevens.

Working at Optus under successive chief executives Chris Anderson and Paul O'Sullivan, and with colleagues like Scott Lorson, Martin Dalgleish and Chris Keely, taught me a great deal about meeting customer needs, including the fundamental human need to connect with others.

Over my time in politics, whether as parliamentary secretary to Malcolm Turnbull tackling online safety, or working closely with Scott Morrison and Josh Frydenberg on the News Media Bargaining Code, I have seen again and again how central the internet is to modern society and modern government.

I could have done none of this without my wife Manuela, whom I thank most of all.

NOTES

1   Australian Bureau of Statistics, 'Household Use of Information Technology', ABS cat. no. 8146.0, 1998, p. 25, https://www.ausstats.abs.gov.au/ausstats/subscriber.nsf/0/CA25687100069892CA2568880027891E/$File/81460_1998.pdf (viewed July 2021).

2   Australian Bureau of Statistics, 'Household Use of Information Technology', ABS cat. no. 8146.0, 2000, p. 5, https://www.ausstats.abs.gov.au/ausstats/subscriber.nsf/0/BB0A2C4391E3FE67CA256A46000801F6/$File/81460_2000.pdf (viewed July 2021).

3   M Roser, H Ritchie and E Ortiz-Ospina, 'Internet', *Our World in Data*, 2015, https://ourworldindata.org/internet (viewed July 2021).

4   L Granwal, 'Smartphone Penetration as Share of the Population in Australia in 2017 with a Forecast until 2025', *Statista*, 8 October 2020, https://www.statista.com/statistics/321477/smartphone-user-penetration-in-australia (viewed July 2021).

5   So called 'cross-platform SMS' was introduced in 1999. This triggered a rapid take-up of SMS; previously, if you were a Vodafone customer, you could send an SMS to another Vodafone customer, but not to someone who

was with Telstra or Optus. Since people generally did not know which of their friends used the same network as they did, people did not use SMS much: see C Erickson, 'Brief History of Text Messaging', *Mashable Australia*, 21 September 2012.

6 S Kemp, 'Digital 2021: April Global Statshot Report', *Datareportal*, 21 April 2021, https://datareportal.com/reports/digital-2021-april-global-statshot (viewed July 2021).

7 Robert J Gordon, *The Rise and Fall of American Growth: the U.S. Standard of Living since the Civil War*, Princeton University Press, Princeton, NJ, 2015, p. x.

8 T McCrann, 'Australia Can't Afford to Lose Battle with Google', *The Australian*, 26 January 2021, p. 53.

9 JP Barlow, 'A Declaration of the Independence of Cyberspace', *Electronic Frontier Foundation*, 8 February 1996, https://www.eff.org/cyberspace-independence (viewed July 2021).

10 Australian Interactive Media Industry Association, 'Enhancing Online Safety for Children', discussion paper submission, Department of Infrastructure, Transport, Regional Development and Communications, 7 March 2014, p. 2, https://www.communications.gov.au/sites/default/files/submissions/Australian_Interactive_Media_Industry_Association.pdf (viewed July 2021).

11 Australian Taxation Office, 'GST on Low Value Imported Goods', https://www.ato.gov.au/Business/International-tax-for-business/GST-on-low-value-imported-goods (viewed July 2021).

12 Australian Competition & Consumer Commission, 'Digital Platforms Inquiry: Final Report', June 2019, p. 6,

https://www.accc.gov.au/systemfiles/Digital%20platforms %20inquiry%20-%20final%20report%20-executive%20 summary.pdf (viewed July 2021).

13 Australian Government, 'Media Reform Green Paper: Modernising Television Regulation in Australia', Department of Infrastructure, Transport, Regional Development and Communications, November 2020, p. 14, https:// www.communications.gov.au/have-your-say/new-rules-new-media-landscape-modernising-television-regulation-australia (viewed July 2021).

14 Australian Competition & Consumer Commission, 'Digital Advertising Services Inquiry: Interim Report', December 2020, https://www.accc.gov.au/system/files/ Digital%20Advertising%20Services%20Inquiry%20-%20 Interim%20report.pdf (viewed July 2021).

15 eSafety Commissioner, 'Image-Based Abuse: Prevalence and Pathways', May 2017, https://www.esafety.gov.au/ about-us/research/image-based-abuse/prevalence-pathways (viewed July 2021).

16 ACCC Scamwatch, 'Scams Cost Australians over $630 million', 22 June 2020, https://www.scamwatch.gov.au/ news-alerts/scams-cost-australians-over-630-million (viewed July 2021).

17 See eSafety Commissioner annual reports: https://www. esafety.gov.au/about-us/corporate-documents/annual-reports (viewed July 2021).

18 Attorneys-General, 'Review of Model Defamation Provisions: Stage 2', NSW Government, 2020, https:// www.justice.nsw.gov.au/justicepolicy/Documents/review-model-defamation-provisions/discussion-paper-stage-2. pdf (viewed July 2021).

19 Australian Communications and Media Authority, 'Digital Platforms Commit to Action on Disinformation', media release, 22 February 2021, https://www.acma.gov.au/articles/2021-02/digital-platforms-commit-action-disinformation (viewed July 2021).

20 eSafety Commissioner, 'Parenting and Pornography: Findings from Australia, New Zealand and the United Kingdom—Summary Report', 10 December 2018, https://www.esafety.gov.au/about-us/research/digital-parenting/pornography (viewed July 2021).

21 Australian Bureau of Statistics, 'Internet Activity, Australia, Dec 2010', 2010, ABS cat. no. 8153.0, https://www.abs.gov.au/AUSSTATS/abs@.nsf/Lookup/8153.0Main+Features1Dec%202010?OpenDocument (viewed July 2021).

22 NBN, 'Report on Assessment Methodology: Extent to Which the NBN Access Network Is Built and Fully Operational', Department of Infrastructure, Transport, Regional Development and Communications, November 2020, p. 65, https://www.communications.gov.au/sites/default/files/report-on-assessment-methodology-extent-nbn-access-network-built-and-operational.pdf (viewed July 2021). See also NBN, 'How We're Tracking: May 2021', May 2021, https://www.nbnco.com.au/corporate-information/about-nbn-co/updates/dashboard-april-2021#2021 (viewed July 2021).

23 Roy Morgan, 'Netflix Is the New Black: 1 Million Users, More than 3 Times Rivals Presto, Stan, Quickflix & Foxtel Play Combined', media release, 23 June 2015, http://www.roymorgan.com/findings/6312-netflix-already-dominates-streaming-video-on-demand-television-may-2015-201506230322 (viewed July 2021).

24 Statistics from OzTAM, https://oztam.com.au/ LatestAvailableReports.aspx (viewed July 2021).

25 *Statista*, 'Penetration Rate of Subscription Video on Demand Services', 2019.

26 Estimate based on a $400 000 variable-interest loan with a remaining period of twenty-five years using the Government's Moneysmart calculator: https:// moneysmart.gov.au/home-loans/mortgage-switching-calculator (viewed July 2021).

27 Alan Noble, 'Australia: From the Consumers to the Creators of Technology', *Google Australia Blog*, 5 June 2012, https://australia.googleblog.com/2012/06/australia-from-consumers-to-creators-of.html (viewed July 2021).

28 B Collins, 'The Atlassian Founders Say the Australian Government Doesn't Understand Tech', *Business Insider Australia*, 26 May 2014, https://www.businessinsider.com. au/the-atlassian-founders-say-the-australian-government-doesnt-understand-tech-2014-5 (viewed July 2021).

29 Daron Acemoglu and James Robinson, *Why Nations Fail: The Origins of Power, Prosperity and Poverty*, Profile Books, London, 2012, p. 217.

30 Australian Bureau of Statistics, 'International Trade in Goods and Services, Australia: Table 12b—Merchandise Exports, Standard International Trade Classification', 2020, https://www.abs.gov.au/statistics/economy/international-trade/international-trade-goods-and-services-australia/ latest-release (viewed July 2021).

31 Glenn Stevens, 'The Challenge of Prosperity', address to the Committee for Economic Development of Australia Annual Dinner, Melbourne, 29 November 2010, https:// www.rba.gov.au/speeches/2010/sp-gov-291110.html (viewed July 2021).

32 IMDb, *Peter Rabbit* (2018), https://www.imdb.com/title/tt5117670 (viewed July 2021); *Happy Feet* (2006), https://www.imdb.com/title/tt0366548 (viewed July 2021).

33 The IF Team, 'Rising Sun Pictures Shares Oscar Nomination for *X-Men: Days of Future Past*', media release, *if.com.au*, 15 January 2015, https://www.if.com.au/rising-sun-pictures-shares-oscar-nomination-for-x-men-days-of-future-past (viewed July 2021).

34 James Caddy, Luc Delaney, Chay Fisher and Clare Noone, 'Consumer Payment Behaviour in Australia', Reserve Bank of Australia, 19 March 2020, https://www.rba.gov.au/publications/bulletin/2020/mar/pdf/consumer-payment-behaviour-in-australia.pdf (viewed July 2021).

35 *The Economist* Intelligence Unit, 'Preparing for Disruption: Technological Readiness Ranking', 2018, http://www.eiu.com/public/thankyou_download.aspx?activity=download&campaignid=techreadiness (viewed July 2021).

36 Tweet from Fawaz Rashed on 19 March 2011, cited in Bani Sapra, 'The Last Decade Showed How Social Media Could Topple Governments and Make Social Change—and It's Only Getting Crazier from Here', *Business Insider Australia*, 14 January 2020, https://www.businessinsider.com.au/social-media-activism-facebook-twitter-youtube-power-2019-12?r=US&IR=T (viewed July 2021).

37 Catherine O'Donnell, 'New Study Quantifies Use of Social Media in Arab Spring', *University of Washington News*, 12 September 2011, https://www.washington.edu/news/2011/09/12/new-study-quantifies-use-of-social-media-in-arab-spring (viewed July 2021).

38 Khaled Koubaa, quoted in Peter Beaumont, 'The Truth about Twitter, Facebook and the Uprisings in the Arab

World', *The Guardian*, 25 February 2011, https://www.theguardian.com/world/2011/feb/25/twitter-facebook-uprisings-arab-libya (viewed July 2021).

39 Matt Reynolds, 'Welcome to E-stonia, the World's Most Digitally Advanced Society', *WIRED*, 20 October 2016, https://www.wired.co.uk/article/digital-estonia (viewed July 2021).

40 United Nations Department of Economic and Social Affairs, 'E-Government Survey 2020: Digital Government in the Decade of Action for Sustainable Development', 2020, https://publicadministration.un.org/egovkb/Portals/egovkb/Documents/un/2020-Survey/2020%20UN%20E-Government%20Survey%20(Full%20Report).pdf (viewed July 2021).

41 International Organization of Motor Vehicle Manufacturers, '2017 Production Statistics', 2017, https://www.oica.net/category/production-statistics (viewed July 2021).

42 Organisation for Economic Co-operation and Development, '130 Countries and Jurisdictions Join Bold New Framework for International Tax Reform', 1 July 2021, https://www.oecd.org/newsroom/130-countries-and-jurisdictions-join-bold-new-framework-for-international-tax-reform.htm (viewed July 2021).